en

ANIMAL ATHLETICS

Isabel Thomas

capstone®

Edited by Linda Staniford
Designed by Steve Mead
Picture research by Kelly Garvin
Production by Victoria Fitzgerald
Originated by Capstone Global Library Ltd
Printed and bound in China
19 18 17 16 15
10 9 8 7 6 5 4 3 2 1

Library of Congress Cataloging-in-Publication Data
Cataloging-in-publication information is on file with the Library of Congress.
Written by Isabel Thomas
ISBN 978-1-4109-8090-8 (hardcover)
ISBN 978-1-4109-8098-4 (eBook PDF)

Acknowledgments
The author and publisher are grateful to the following for permission to reproduce copyright material:
Corbis/Stephen Krasemann/All Canada Photos, 16; Getty Images: Al Tielemans/Sports Illustrated, 10, Bill Frakes/Sports Illustrated, 6, Stu Forster, 18; Glow Images/DLILLC/Corbis, 25; iStockphoto/Dirk Freder, 26; Minden Pictures: Atsuo Fujimaru, 13, Konrad Wothe, 8, Satoshi Kuribayashi, cover (top left), Stephen Dalton, 13, 20, ZSSD, 24; Newscom: Davy Adam/PA Photos/ABACA, 4, Gerard Lacz/VWPics, 7, Julian Stratenschulte/dpa/picture-alliance, 27, Kieran Galvin/Actionplus, 22, Mark Blinch/Rueters, 14, Matthias Breiter/Minden Pictures, 12, Michael Durham/Minden Pictures, 19, Wil Meinderts/Buiten-beeld/Minden Pictures, 23; Shutterstock: Cat Downie, 5, kingfisher, 9, paula french, 17, 31, Sekar B, 11, Stuart G. Porter, cover (bottom), Suede Chen, 9, Wolfgang Zwanzger, cover (top right); Superstock: Jurgen Feuerer/age footstock, 15; Wikimedia/Brain Gratwicke, 21

Artistic Elements: Shutterstock: Elena Paletskaya, kavalenkava volha, kotss, La Gorda, mazura1989, Nikiteev_Konstantin, PinkPueblo, Potapov Alexander, Stockobaza, yyang.

We would like to thank Michael Bright for his help in the preparation of this book.

Every effort has been made to contact copyright holders of any material reproduced in this book. Any omissions will be rectified in subsequent printings if notice is given to the publisher.

All the Internet addresses (URLs) given in this book were valid at the time of going to press. However, due to the dynamic nature of the Internet, some addresses may have changed, or sites may have changed or ceased to exist since publication. While the author and publisher regret any inconvenience this may cause readers, no responsibility for any such changes can be accepted by either the author or the publisher.

007494CTPSS16

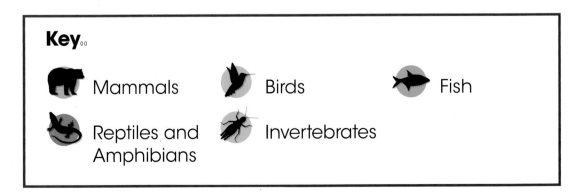

Key 00

Mammals

Birds

Fish

Reptiles and Amphibians

Invertebrates

CONTENTS

LET THE GAMES BEGIN! 4

EVENT 1: SPRINT 6

EVENT 2: HIGH JUMP 10

EVENT 3: MARATHON 14

EVENT 4: LONG JUMP 18

EVENT 5: SHOT PUT 22

AMAZING ADAPTATIONS 26

MEDAL TABLE 28

GLOSSARY 30

FIND OUT MORE 31

INDEX 32

Some words are shown in bold, **like this**. You can find out what they mean by looking in the glossary.

LET THE GAMES BEGIN!

Every four years, the Olympic Games test the speed, skill, and strength of the world's best athletes. **Athletics** are the track and field events that take place inside the Olympic stadium. These include running, jumping, and throwing competitions.

In any forest, ocean, or grassland, you'll find animals that could beat the best human athletes. Speed, jumping, and throwing skills are all **adaptations** that help animals to **survive**. Let's find out which animal athletes deserve a medal at the Animalympics!

SPRINT

The 100-meter sprint is one of the oldest Olympic sports. Winners have been recorded since the ancient Olympic Games, which were held more than 2,800 years ago! Today's top **competitors** can run the length of a football field in just under 10 seconds. But this is slow compared to the fastest animal athletes.

Spiked shoes help runners grip the track.

🐻 Cheetah

Scientists tracked cheetahs in Botswana and found they could run at up to 58 miles (93 kilometers) per hour. At this speed, they'd cross the finish line for the 100-meter sprint in less than six seconds!

Cheetahs sprint around 558 feet (170 meters) each time they hunt their speedy **prey**. They don't stay at their top speed for long.

Peregrine falcon

If the 100-meter sprint were held in the air, the Peregrine falcon would win. No animal can move faster than this bird diving to grab its **prey**. A top speed of almost 242 miles (390 kilometers) per hour lets this bird of prey travel 328 feet (100 meters) in less than a second!

wings tucked close to body

At top speed an Australian tiger beetle like this one can run 170 body lengths per second!

Southern Californian desert mite

For a long time, scientists thought this Australian tiger beetle was the world's fastest animal for its size. Then they discovered a tiny southern Californian desert mite that zooms along at 322 body lengths per second! The fastest human sprinters only travel six times their body length every second.

HIGH JUMP

Human high jumpers must take off from one foot and soar across the bar without knocking it to the ground. By turning their bodies and arching their backs, top jumpers can clear almost 8 feet (2.5 meters), the height of a soccer goal.

bar

arched back

foam bed

 **Salmon**

Some fish can out-jump humans. Before salmon **breed**, they swim from the ocean back to the river where they hatched. This is often a difficult journey. In some rivers, salmon must leap up waterfalls almost 13 feet (4 meters) high.

churning water gives salmon a boost

🐻 Puma

Big cats are the highest-jumping mammals. Pumas can jump up to a cliff ledge or branch nearly 18 feet (5.4 meters) above the ground— more than twice as high as the 8-foot (2.45-meter) human record. A cliff ledge or tree is a safe place to sleep or eat, away from hungry food thieves.

Pumas could leap onto the roof of a two-story house!

 Froghopper

To leap into the air, human high jumpers push against the ground with a **force** two or three times their body weight. A froghopper can push with a force 400 times its body weight, catapulting it 27.5 inches (70 centimeters) into the air. This is like a human leaping 656 feet (200 meters).

MARATHON

The marathon is the longest Olympic running race. Top athletes can complete the 26-mile (42-kilometer) course in two hours, but this would just be a warm-up for the top animal long distance runners.

water stop

 # Camel

Camels' bodies are **adapted** for long journeys in the hottest and driest areas of the world. Camels can go for several days without needing to drink. Their ability to cope with heat and thirst means that they can run for more than 18 hours without stopping!

The hump stores fat, which the camel's body breaks down to get energy and water.

long legs

Pronghorn

Pronghorn, or American antelope, have **adapted** to run fast over long distances. They need to outrun speedy **predators** such as big cats. Pronghorn have been tracked running 6.8 miles (11 kilometers) in just 10 minutes! A cheetah has a higher top speed, but it gets tired much more quickly.

long, thin legs

Even a two-week-old pronghorn can outrun a human!

 # Ostrich

Ostriches can't fly away from danger. Instead, they run on land. Long legs and springy joints mean ostriches use far less energy than humans as they run. An ostrich could complete a 26-mile (42-kilometer) Olympic marathon in just 50 minutes!

claw digs into the ground for grip

16-foot (5-meter) strides

17

LONG JUMP

A 98.5-foot (30-meter) run-up helps Olympic long jumpers take off at high speed. They try to travel as far forward as possible before crash landing in the sand. Top athletes can jump almost 30 feet (9 meters)—the length of five adult bicycles lined up end to end!

sandpit

🐻 Kangaroo rat

Many animals, such as tigers and kangaroos, can leap farther than humans. But the kangaroo rat wins the medal for the mammals. These rodents can jump 20 times their body length, while humans only manage five.

long tail for balance

huge hind feet

Large leaps help kangaroo rats escape **predators** such as snakes.

Jumping spider

Jumping spiders don't spin webs to catch food—they leap on it instead. The two large eyes on the front of the spider's head help it to judge distance. It can make huge leaps up to 40 times its body length.

Six smaller eyes help this jumping spider to spot **prey** moving to its side, and even behind it.

 Tree frog

Tree frogs are the champion amphibian jumpers. An average Australian rocket frog jump is 4 feet (1.2 meters) long, but these tiny frogs can leap up to 13 feet (4 meters)—55 times their body length—to escape from **predators**.

long, powerful legs

rocket-shaped snout

Event 5   SHOT PUT

Humans are the best throwers in the animal kingdom. Our eyes, shoulders, and hands are **adapted** to help us throw all kinds of objects long distances, in the correct direction! In Olympic shot put competitions, athletes hold a heavy metal ball and turn quickly to "put" the "shot" as far as they can.

metal shot

Coconut crab

Coconut crabs can carry a coconut up a tree and throw it back to the ground. The broken coconut is much easier to open and eat. But since they are using **gravity** to boost their throws, coconut crabs only get the bronze!

powerful legs

The shot thrown by human athletes weighs 8.8 pounds (4 kilograms)— as much as a typical pumpkin!

Egyptian vulture

When Egyptian vultures spot a tasty ostrich egg, they look for a smooth, rounded stone. They pick up the stone in their beak and throw it at the egg until the thick shell cracks open. Only half of their shots actually hit the eggs!

ostrich egg

Scientists think the vultures once threw the eggs themselves.

🐻 Chimpanzees

Chimpanzees throw all sorts of things, from stones to poop! They have even been seen collecting objects to throw in the future—showing that just like humans, chimps can plan ahead.

A short thumb means that chimpanzees lose their grip on objects as they swing their arm forward. Human hands have much longer thumbs, which help us to grip objects firmly and throw farther and faster than any other animal.

AMAZING ADAPTATIONS

Animals don't run, jump, or throw objects as a sport. The body features that make animals good at running fast, jumping high, or throwing well have **adapted** over thousands of years to help them **survive** in certain habitats.

These features help animals to find food, attract mates, care for their young, or avoid getting eaten. This means they will get passed on to the next **generation**.

Watching record-breaking animal athletes helps scientists find out how animal bodies work. This information is used in amazing ways, such as designing robots that can move using as little energy as possible.

Springs in this Bionic Kangaroo's legs store energy between jumps, just like the **tendons** of a real kangaroo.

MEDAL TABLE

It's time for the Animalympic medal ceremony! The animal kingdom is divided into groups. Animals with similar features belong to the same class. Which class will take home the most medals for **athletics**?

Mammals

Mammals are warm-blooded animals that have hair or fur and feed milk to their young. They live on land or in water, and range in size from a bumble-bee-sized bat to a blue whale, the largest animal on Earth!

Reptiles and Amphibians

Reptiles and amphibians are cold-blooded animals, which means they rely on the Sun's energy to stay warm. Reptiles have dry, scaly skin. Amphibians have moist, smooth skin.

Birds

Birds have feathers, wings, and a beak. Most birds can fly, but how will they perform on the running track?

Invertebrates

This group includes all animals without a backbone, such as insects, spiders, and snails. Many have a skeleton on the outside of their bodies instead.

Fish

Fish live in saltwater or freshwater. They have fins for swimming and gills to breathe underwater.

RESULTS

EVENT	3 BRONZE	2 SILVER	1 GOLD
SPRINT	Cheetah	Peregrine falcon	Southern Californian desert mite
HIGH JUMP	Salmon	Puma	Froghopper
MARATHON	Camel	Pronghorn	Ostrich
LONG JUMP	Kangaroo rat	Jumping spider	Tree frog
SHOT PUT	Coconut crab	Egyptian vulture	Chimpanzee

ANIMAL	RANK	GOLD	SILVER	BRONZE
Fish	1	🥇🥇	🥈	🥉
Birds	2	🥇	🥈🥈	🥉🥉🥉
Mammals	3	🥇	🥈🥈	
Reptiles and amphibians	4	🥇		
Invertebrates	5			🥉

GLOSSARY

adaptation change to the body, workings, or behavior of a living thing that makes it better suited to its habitat

adapted changed to be better suited for an environment

athletics group of sports that include running, jumping, and throwing events

breed mate with another animal to produce offspring (babies)

competitor person taking part in a sports match or contest

force push or pull

generation group of living things that were born, or are living, at about the same time

gravity force that pulls objects down toward the ground

predator animal that hunts and kills other animals for food

prey animal that is hunted and killed by another animal for food

survive stay alive

tendon bendable tissue that joins bones to muscles

FIND OUT MORE

Books

Gifford, Clive. *Track Athletics* (Know Your Sport). Mankato, Minn.: Sea-to-Sea, 2009.

Murphy, Julie. *Amazing Animal Adaptations* series. Mankato, Minn.: Capstone, 2012.

Internet sites

Facthound offers a safe, fun way to find Internet sites related to this book. All of the sites on Facthound have been researched by our staff.

Here's all you do:
Visit www.facthound.com
Type in this code: 9781410980908

INDEX

adapt 15, 16, 22
adaptations 5, 26
amphibians 21, 28

birds 8, 17, 24, 28

camel 15
cheetah 7, 16
chimpanzee 25
coconut crab 23

Egyptian vulture 24

fish 11, 28
froghopper 13

high jump 10

invertebrates 9, 13, 20, 23, 28

jumping events 10, 18
jumping spider 20

kangaroo rat 19

long jump 18

mammals 7, 12, 15, 16, 19, 25, 28
marathon 14

ostrich 17

peregrine falcon 8
pronghorn 16
puma 12

running events 6, 14

salmon 11
shot put 22
southern Californian desert mite 9
sprint 6

throwing events 22
tiger beetle 9
tree frog 21